# MINI PIES

# MINI PIES

*Adorably Delicious Recipes
for Your Favorite Treats*

CHRISTY BEAVER *&* MORGAN GREENSETH

**Ulysses Press**

Published by:
Ulysses Press
P.O. Box 3440
Berkeley, CA 94703
www.ulyssespress.com

ISBN: 978-1-56975-980-6
Library of Congress Catalog Number 2011926031

Printed in the United States by Bang Printing

10 9 8 7 6 5 4 3 2 1

Acquisitions editor: Kelly Reed
Managing editor: Claire Chun
Editor: Phyllis Elving
Proofreader: Lauren Harrison
Interior photographs: © Judi Swinks Photography except pages 12–15, 17, 19, 26–27, 29, 122–23, 125 © Lily Chou and page 126 © Candace Shankel
Cover photographs: © Judi Swinks Photography
Design: what!design @ whatweb.com

Distributed by Publishers Group West

*To our mothers and grandmothers,*
*who taught us how sweet life can be.*

# TABLE OF CONTENTS

## NUT & SAVORY PIES

◇◇◇◇◇◇◇◇◇◇◇◇◇◇◇◇◇◇◇

## TOPPINGS

◇◇◇◇◇◇◇◇◇◇◇◇◇◇◇◇◇◇◇

# INTRODUCTION

In the fall of 2009, we were discussing the approaching holidays over pumpkin beers when the subject of baking came up. We agreed there was a void in the baked goods business in the Pacific Northwest: No one makes pies anymore.

It's understandable. Pies are intimidating, and they're something Grandma makes with an ancient recipe and a hundred years of trial and error. A great crust can be tricky, and the filling must be perfect. We were also interested in the emerging mini desserts movement. Cupcakes, scones, and cookies had all been miniaturized, and we decided it was time for pie to get its day in the tiny sun. With a toast and a handshake, Mini Empire Bakery was born and pie miniaturization began.

No dessert has more range than pie. From arriving at a picnic with a fresh batch of pink lemonade pies to curling up with a warm and comforting raspberry rhubarb whiskey pie à la mode, there's a perfect pie for every occasion. This delightful little book contains 25 recipes for both traditional and innovative mini pies. We cover everything from a variety of pie crusts and fillings to tools and techniques. These mini pies are great for parties, potlucks, or any other event. They make excellent party favors, thank-you gifts, and birthday presents.

We live for pie and want to remove the intimidation that surrounds baking it. Our goal is to make it accessible and easy for everyone. We've also included recipes for bakers with vegan and gluten-free dietary restrictions.

Raised in the South and the Midwest, we've both had a passion for baking from a very young age. Our mothers and grandmothers trained us to help in the kitchen as soon as we could walk. From those beginnings developed a lifelong interest. Baking is love. We bake for those that we cherish. Baking is taking time, making effort, and exercising precision to create treats for others. And it's all worth it. A gift in its truest form.

We hope that this book enables you to develop new baking skills, try new flavors, and explore the wonderful world of mini pies.

Sweetest regards,
Christy Beaver and
Morgan Greenseth

# PIE CRUSTS

The crust can make or break a pie. It needs to be just the right combination of flaky, crumbly, salty, and sweet. Luckily for you, we've already figured out how to achieve a heavenly crust for your perfect pie. (You're welcome.)

# PIE CRUST BASICS

Pie crust rolls out best when the dough is slightly cooler than room temperature. If it seems too firm, let it sit on the counter a bit before you roll it. The dough should be pliable and slightly elastic.

*To roll out your crust*, it is essential that you have a generous amount of flour on both your work surface and your rolling pin.

*To cut the crusts* for our mini pies, we use a 4-inch-diameter tart cutter with fluted edges, but any 4-inch round cookie cutter can be used.

Our mini pies are made in muffin tins. *To shape the crust*, place it over a well in the muffin tin and very gently press down in the center until it's almost touching the pan bottom. Then gently press the crust against the sides of the well. Press lightly against the bottom and sides to make sure the crust is formed perfectly to the pan. Check for tears or holes—if you find one, you can patch it by squeezing the dough back together to cover the gap. If your pan has been greased adequately, this shouldn't create a problem.

*For crusts that are baked before being filled,* use this technique:

Cut out the crusts as usual. Working on a floured surface, tap around the edge of each crust with the heel of your hand to stretch it slightly.

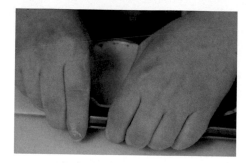

Gently pierce the bottom of the crust with a fork to keep large bubbles from forming, which would also cut down on your filling capacity.

When you shape the crust into the muffin tin, fold the stretched edges out over the horizontal surface of the pan top. This will keep the crust from shrinking during baking, leaving more room for delicious filling.

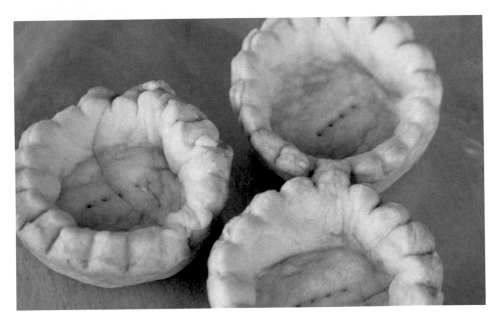

All these dough recipes make enough for 12 mini pies and pie toppers. Leftover dough can be double-wrapped in plastic wrap and refrigerated for 1 week or frozen for up to 3 weeks.

To assure yourself of a crust that bakes to a nice golden brown, brush it with soy milk and sprinkle it with sugar before baking.

How do you know when your pie is done? The crust will be golden, and your kitchen will smell like pie!

# PERFECT PIE CRUST

8 tablespoons
butter (1 stick)

6 tablespoons
shortening

2½ cups all-
purpose flour

2 teaspoons salt

4 teaspoons sugar

6 to 8 tablespoons
ice water

**SWEET TIPS**: *This
recipe makes enough
dough for 12 mini pies
and pie toppers.*

*Leftover dough can
be double wrapped
in plastic wrap and
refrigerated for 1
week, or frozen for
up to 3 weeks.*

1. Chop the butter and shortening into ¼-inch pieces. Place in the freezer to chill while you prepare the other ingredients.

2. Blend the flour, salt, and sugar in a food processor. Add the chilled shortening and process until the mixture climbs the walls of the processor bowl. Add the butter, one piece at a time, and process thoroughly.

3. Add the ice water 1 tablespoon at a time until the mixture comes together in a ball and makes 2 laps around the processor bowl.

4. Remove the dough, divide it in half, and flatten each half into a disc. Wrap each disc in plastic wrap and chill in the refrigerator for 30 minutes.

# GRAHAM CRACKER PIE CRUST

8 tablespoons butter (1 stick)

6 tablespoons shortening

2 cups all-purpose flour

½ cup fine graham cracker crumbs (processed until they look like sand), plus more for rolling out the dough

2 teaspoons salt

4 teaspoons sugar

5 to 6 tablespoons ice water

SWEET TIPS: *We prefer cinnamon graham crackers for this recipe.*

1. Chop the butter and shortening into ¼-inch pieces. Place in the freezer to chill while you prepare the other ingredients.

2. In a food processor, blend the flour, ½ cup graham cracker crumbs, salt, and sugar. Add the shortening and process until the mixture climbs the walls of the processor bowl. Add the butter one piece at a time and process thoroughly.

3. Add the ice water 1 tablespoon at a time until the mixture comes together in a ball and makes 2 laps around the processor bowl. Remove the dough, divide it in half, and flatten each half into a disc. Wrap each disc in plastic wrap and chill in the refrigerator for 30 minutes.

4. Before rolling out the dough, generously coat your work surface with both flour and graham cracker crumbs. The crumbs will coat the outside of each mini pie, adding flavor and giving the look of a traditional graham cracker crust.

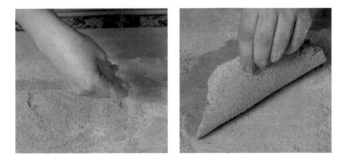

# VEGAN PIE CRUST

8 tablespoons vegan margarine (we like Earth Balance vegan buttery sticks)

6 tablespoons vegan shortening (we like Earth Balance vegan shortening sticks)

2½ cups all-purpose flour

2 teaspoons salt

4 teaspoons sugar

6 to 8 tablespoons ice water

SWEET TIPS: *Grease the muffin tins for vegan pies with the vegan buttery sticks.*

*All of our fruit pie fillings are vegan friendly; use this crust recipe for any of them.*

1. Chop the margarine and shortening into ¼-inch pieces. Place in the freezer to chill while you prepare the other ingredients.

2. In a food processor, blend the flour, salt, and sugar. Add the shortening and process until the mixture climbs the walls of the processor bowl. Add the butter one piece at a time and process thoroughly.

3. Add the ice water 1 tablespoon at a time until the mixture comes together in a ball and makes 2 laps around the processor bowl. Remove the dough from the processor bowl, divide in half, and flatten each half into a disc. Wrap each disc in plastic wrap and chill in the refrigerator for 30 minutes.

# NUTTY PIE CRUST

1. Combine the coconut oil and maple syrup in a small bowl.

2. In a food processor, blend the ground nuts, gluten-free flour, sugar, baking powder, and salt.

3. With the processor running, gradually add the maple syrup mixture and process until the dough comes together in a ball and makes 2 laps around processor bowl. Remove the dough from the processor, divide it in half, and flatten each half into a disc. Wrap each disc in plastic wrap and chill in the refrigerator for 30 minutes.

3 tablespoons melted coconut oil

¾ cup pure maple syrup

1 cup finely ground pecans (or other nuts), ground in a food processor

3¼ cups gluten-free flour, such as rice flour

2 tablespoons sugar

¼ teaspoon baking powder

Pinch of salt

**SWEET TIPS**: *This spin on traditional crust is deliciously gluten-free. This is a very sticky dough. To make rolling out the crusts easier and less messy, place the dough between two pieces of wax paper.*

# GLUTEN-FREE
# PIE CRUST

‹❖❖❖❖❖❖❖❖❖❖❖❖❖❖❖❖❖❖❖❖❖›

1¼ cups plus 2 tablespoons palm oil

2½ cups rice flour

½ cup almond meal

¼ teaspoon salt

6 tablespoons honey

½ teaspoon almond extract

3 tablespoons ice water

**SWEET TIPS**: *This crust needs to be prebaked for 10 to 15 minutes at 350°F before you fill your mini pies; follow the directions on page 14.*

*Because of the honey and almonds, this crust is better with sweet pies than with savory.*

1. Using an electric mixer, beat the palm oil until softened.

2. In a food processor, blend the rice flour, almond meal, and salt. With the processor running, slowly add the palm oil until completely mixed.

3. Add the honey, almond extract, and water until the mixture comes together in a ball and makes 2 laps around the processor bowl. Remove the dough from the processor, divide in half, and flatten each half into a disc. Wrap each disc in plastic wrap and keep in a cool place. If you're not using the crust right away, keep it in the refrigerator. Otherwise refrigeration is not necessary.

# CHEDDAR CHEESE PIE CRUST

1. Chop the butter and shortening into ¼-inch pieces. Place in the freezer to chill while you prepare the other ingredients.

2. In a food processor, blend the flour, salt, and sugar. Add the shortening and process until the mixture climbs the walls of the processor bowl. Add the cheese and process until blended. Add the butter one piece at a time and process thoroughly.

3. Add the ice water 1 tablespoon at a time until the mixture comes together in a ball and makes 2 laps around the processor bowl. Remove the dough from the processor, divide it in half, and flatten each half into a disc. Wrap each disc in plastic wrap and chill in the refrigerator for 30 minutes.

8 tablespoons butter (1 stick)

3 tablespoons shortening

2½ cups all-purpose flour

2 teaspoons salt

4 teaspoons sugar

½ cup grated sharp Cheddar cheese

6 to 8 tablespoons ice water

**SWEET TIPS**: *This recipe makes enough dough for 12 mini pies and pie toppers.*

*This crust is great to use for any savory pie or mini quiche.*

# SHORTBREAD PIE CRUST

10 tablespoons
butter (1¼ sticks)

2⅓ cups all-
purpose flour

½ cup sugar

1 teaspoon salt

½ teaspoon
baking powder

¼ cup heavy
whipping cream

1 egg

1 teaspoon
vanilla extract

**SWEET TIPS**: *This
delightful crust can be
challenging. If you roll
out the crust and it's
too crumbly, use your
hands to knead it back
into a ball and then roll
it out again. The dough
will be more elastic the
second time around.*

*If a shortbread cookie and a perfect pie crust had a love
child, this would be it.*

1. Chop the butter into ¼-inch pieces. Place in the
freezer to chill while you prepare the other ingredients.

2. In a food processor, blend the flour, sugar, and
salt. Add the butter a few pieces at a time and process until the mixture looks like sand.

3. In a bowl, gently whisk together the cream, egg,
and vanilla.

4. With the food processor running, add the cream
mixture in a steady stream until the dough comes
together in a ball and makes 2 laps around the
processor bowl. Remove the dough from the processor, divide it in half, and flatten each half into
a disc. Wrap each disc in plastic wrap and chill in
the refrigerator for 1 hour.

# PIE IN A JAR

*Christy's best friend, Samie, thinks this is the best thing since sliced bread.*

We like to assemble pies in half-pint Mason jars and freeze them to bake later. Here's how you do that. Each recipe in this book will make about 3 mini Mason jar pies. This technique works with any of the fruit pie recipes or with our Bourbon Pecan pie.

## Assembling the pies:

1. Prepare your chosen pie filling and set it aside.

2. Generously coat the insides of the Mason jars with cooking spray.

3. Working on a thoroughly floured surface, roll out the crust to a thickness of 3/16 inch. Using an inverted 6-inch-diameter bowl as your "cutter," cut out 3 crusts with a knife.

Pie filling

3 wide-mouth, half-pint Mason jars, with lids

Perfect Pie Crust (recipe on page 16)

6-inch-diameter bowl for cutting out the crusts

**SWEET TIPS**: *We believe that there are few things on this earth better than warm pie with cold ice cream, so be sure to keep some ice cream on hand to serve with your mini Mason jar pies.*

3. For each pie, take a 6-inch circle of crust and drape it over the top of a jar. Lift up the crust edges and gently press down on the center of the dough circle until it reaches the bottom of the jar. Now press the sides of the crust against the sides of the jar.

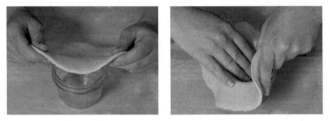

Make sure the crust is touching the jar on all surfaces. If the crust extends above the top edge of the jar, trim it with a knife.

4. Spoon in the filling to ½ inch below the jar rim.

5. You have the option here of adding a top crust.
To do this, use your 4-inch-diameter round cutter
to cut out a circle of dough. Then take your favorite
decorative mini cutter and press out a little hole
right in the middle of the crust circle. Place this
crust on top of the filling in the jar, pressing around
the edges to seal the top and bottom crusts together.
Keep in mind that the lid has to fasten onto the
jar—adjust your filling and crust accordingly.

**6.** Screw on the lids, label each jar with the pie flavor, and put in the freezer for up to 3 months.

## Baking the pies:

1. Take the Mason jar out of the freezer, remove the lid, and let sit at room temperature for about an hour so the jar can come closer to room temperature. (You can let your pie thaw while you prepare dinner.)

2. Preheat the oven to 375°F.

3. Place the pie jar on a rimmed baking sheet and bake for 45 minutes with the lid off, until the crust is browned and your kitchen smells like pie.

4. Remove the pie from the oven and let cool for at least 15 minutes. (We know it's tough, but don't dive right into the boiling-hot pie.)

5. Enjoy right out of the jar! Each pie jar is just right for two people to share (or to keep all to yourself).

# FRUIT PIES

Fruit pies are always a hit. Who doesn't like sweet cherry pie on a summer day? These pies are easy for the novice baker, or anyone who knows their way around the produce section. You can just make your friends think that you were in the kitchen all day, when actually it took no time at all.

# SWEETHEART CHERRY

1 pound fresh sweet cherries, pitted and diced in ½-inch pieces

¼ cup sugar, plus extra for sprinkling

½ tablespoon cornstarch

1 tablespoon lemon juice

Perfect Pie Crust (recipe on page 16)

¼ cup soy milk

*A nice treat for your sweetheart. Or just for you.*

1. Preheat the oven to 350°F. Generously grease a 12-cup muffin tin with butter or cooking spray.

2. Combine the cherries, ¼ cup sugar, cornstarch, and lemon juice in a large bowl.

3. On a thoroughly floured surface, roll out the pie crust to a thickness of $\frac{3}{16}$ inch. Using a 4-inch-diameter round cutter, cut 12 crusts. Re-form and re-roll the dough as necessary, keeping plenty of flour on your work surface.

4. Using a mini cookie cutter (your choice) and leftover dough, cut out 12 shapes to use as pie toppers. (We like to use hearts for Sweetheart Cherry pie.)

5. Carefully shape the crusts into the wells of the muffin tin, crimping the edges with your fingers.

6. Fill each mini pie with 1½ tablespoons of the cherry mixture. Be careful not to put too much

juice in with the cherries, or they are likely to bubble over. Top each mini pie with a pie topper.

**7.** With a pastry brush, lightly brush the pie crusts with soy milk, then sprinkle with sugar.

**8.** Bake for 20 to 25 minutes, until the crusts are golden brown. Allow to cool for a few minutes in the muffin tin, then carefully remove the pies from the tin and place on a wire rack to finish cooling. To remove, first try to spin the pies in the muffin wells. If they need a little extra help, run a butter knife along the edge of the crusts to pop them out of the tin.

**9.** Serve, or store in an airtight container at room temperature for up to 2 days.

# BLUEBERRY– ROSE WATER

*Your friends will be really impressed by the fact that you know what rose water is.*

1. Preheat the oven to 350°F. Generously grease a 12-cup muffin tin with butter or cooking spray.

2. Combine the blueberries, ¼ cup sugar, cinnamon, rose water, and lemon juice in a large bowl.

3. On a thoroughly floured surface, roll out the pie crust to a thickness of ³⁄₁₆ inch. Using a 4-inch-diameter round cutter, cut 12 crusts. Re-form and re-roll the dough as necessary, keeping plenty of flour on your work surface.

4. Using a mini cookie cutter (your choice) and leftover dough, cut out 12 shapes to use as pie toppers. (We like to use bluebirds for Blueberry–Rose Water pie.)

5. Carefully shape the crusts into the wells of the muffin tin, crimping the edges with your fingers.

3 cups blueberries

¼ cup sugar, plus extra for sprinkling

¼ teaspoon ground cinnamon

1 tablespoon culinary rose water

1 tablespoon lemon juice

Perfect Pie Crust (recipe on page 16)

¼ cup soy milk

6. Fill each mini pie to the brim with the blueberry mixture, about 2 tablespoons for each pie. Top each mini pie with a pie topper.

7. With a pastry brush, lightly brush the pie crusts with soy milk, then sprinkle with sugar.

8. Bake for 20 to 25 minutes, until the crusts are golden brown. Allow to cool for a few minutes in the muffin tin, then carefully remove the pies from the pan and place on a wire rack to finish cooling. To remove, first try to spin the pies in the muffin wells. If they need a little extra help, run a butter knife along the edge of the crusts to pop them out of the tin.

9. Serve, or store in an airtight container at room temperature for up to 2 days.

SWEET TIPS: *Rose water can be found at natural food stores and specialty grocery stores. Make sure that you purchase the kind meant for cooking, containing no glycerin.*

# VERRY BERRY

1 cup blackberries

½ cup blueberries

1¼ cups strawberries

¾ cup raspberries

½ cup fresh or frozen cranberries

¼ cup sugar, plus extra for sprinkling

1 tablespoon lemon juice

½ teaspoon ground cinnamon

½ tablespoon cornstarch

Perfect Pie Crust (recipe on page 16)

¼ cup soy milk

*All the sweetness of summer, condensed into one delicious little pie.*

1. Preheat the oven to 350°F. Generously grease a 12-cup muffin tin with butter or cooking spray.

2. Chop all the fruits into ¼-inch pieces; the cranberries and blueberries should all be cut in half in the chopping process.

3. Combine the berries, ¼ cup sugar, lemon juice, cinnamon, and cornstarch in a large bowl. Let sit for 30 minutes to allow the berry flavors to blend.

4. On a thoroughly floured surface, roll out the crust to a thickness of 3/16 inch. Using a 4-inch-diameter round cutter, cut 12 crusts. Re-form and re-roll the dough as necessary, keeping plenty of flour on your work surface.

5. Using a mini cookie cutter (your choice) and leftover dough, cut out 12 shapes to use as pie toppers. (We like mini strawberry shapes—pierced with

a fork before baking for added detail—for our Verry Berry pie.)

6. Carefully shape the crusts into the wells of the muffin tin, crimping the edges with your fingers.

7. Fill each mini pie with 2 tablespoons of the berry mixture. Don't include too much of the juice, as this filling is prone to boiling over. Top each mini pie with a pie topper.

8. With a pastry brush, lightly brush the pie crusts with soy milk, then sprinkle with sugar.

9. Bake for 20 to 25 minutes, until the crusts are golden brown. Allow to cool for a few minutes in the muffin tin, then carefully remove the pies from the pan and place on a wire rack to finish cooling. To remove, first try to spin the pies in the muffin wells. If they need a little extra help, run a butter knife along the edge of the crusts to pop them out of the tin.

10. Serve, or store in an airtight container at room temperature for up to 2 days.

SWEET TIPS: *Fresh berries are the very best, but frozen ones also work well. The blackberries and raspberries tend to burst while these pies are baking, so beware of overfilling.*

# SWEET STRAWBERRY
## with Basil Whipped Cream

Basil Whipped Cream
(recipe on page 120)

4 cups fresh
strawberries, diced
into ¼-inch pieces

¼ cup sugar

1 tablespoon cornstarch

Perfect Pie Crust
(recipe on page 16)

*Yep, you heard us right.*

1. Begin making the Basil Whipped Cream far enough ahead of time that the cream can be chilled and infused with the flavor of the basil for 2 hours (see Step 1 on page 120).

2. Preheat the oven to 350°F. Generously grease a 12-cup muffin tin with butter or cooking spray.

3. Combine the diced strawberries, sugar, and cornstarch in a bowl.

4. On a thoroughly floured surface, roll out the pie crust to a thickness of ³⁄₁₆ inch. Using a 4-inch-diameter round cutter, cut 12 crusts. Re-form and re-roll the dough as necessary, keeping plenty of flour on your work surface.

5. Carefully shape the crusts into the wells of the muffin tin, crimping the edges with your fingers.

**6.** Fill each mini pie to the brim with 3 tablespoons of the strawberry mixture. Don't include too much of the liquid, as this filling is prone to boiling over.

**7.** Bake for 30 minutes, until the crusts are golden brown. Allow to cool for a few minutes in the muffin tin, then carefully remove the pies from the pan and place on a wire rack to finish cooling. To remove, first try to spin the pies in the muffin wells. If they need a little extra help, run a butter knife along the edge of the crusts to pop them out of the tin.

**8.** While your pies are in the oven, continue making the Basil Whipped Cream (Steps 2 and 3 on page 120). Spoon the finished whipped cream into a pastry bag.

**9.** When the pies have cooled completely, pipe a hefty serving of Basil Whipped Cream onto each pie. Serve, or refrigerate in an airtight container for up to 2 days.

# RASPBERRY RHUBARB WHISKEY

*In case you've ever wondered what you can do with rhubarb.*

1. Combine the rhubarb, 1½ cups raspberries, honey, whiskey, and ¼ cup sugar in a medium-size saucepan. Cook over medium heat just until the rhubarb is tender but not mushy, gently stirring occasionally. Allow to cool completely, then use a strainer to remove the liquid.

2. Preheat the oven to 350°F. Generously grease a 12-cup muffin tin with butter or cooking spray.

3. On a thoroughly floured surface, roll out the crust to a thickness of ³⁄₁₆ inch. Using a 4-inch-diameter round cutter, cut 12 crusts. Re-form and re-roll dough as necessary, keeping plenty of flour on your work surface.

4. Using a mini cookie cutter (your choice) and leftover dough, cut out 12 shapes to use as pie toppers. (We like to use hearts on our Raspberry Rhubarb Whiskey pie.)

2½ cups rhubarb, chopped into ½-inch pieces

2½ cups raspberries, divided

2 tablespoons honey

2 tablespoons whiskey

¼ cup sugar, plus extra for sprinkling

Perfect Pie Crust (recipe on page 16)

¼ cup soy milk

**SWEET TIPS:** *If you have an ice cream maker, you can use the liquid you strained off from the rhubarb filling to make a batch of incredible sorbet. Or use it for homemade popsicles or to spike/flavor iced tea.*

5. Carefully shape the crusts into the wells of the muffin tin, crimping the edges with your fingers.

6. Place 3 or 4 fresh raspberries in each crust. Then fill each mini pie with 1½ tablespoons of the rhubarb mixture. Don't include too much of the juice with the filling, as this pie is prone to boiling over. Top each mini pie with a pie topper.

7. With a pastry brush, lightly brush the pie crusts with soy milk, then sprinkle with sugar.

8. Bake for 20 to 25 minutes, until the crusts are golden brown. Allow to cool for a few minutes in the muffin tin, then carefully remove the pies from the pan and place on a wire rack to finish cooling. To remove, first try to spin the pies in the muffin wells. If they need a little extra help, run a butter knife along the edge of the crusts to pop them out of the tin.

9. Serve, or store in an airtight container at room temperature for up to 2 days.

# ABC PIE

1 apple, peeled, cored, and diced in ¼-inch pieces (we like Granny Smith for this pie)

½ cup blackberries, fresh or frozen

1 cup sweet cherries, pitted and sliced in half

⅓ cup sugar, plus extra for sprinkling

2 tablespoons cornstarch

½ tablespoon lemon juice

½ teaspoon vanilla extract

¼ teaspoon ground cinnamon

Perfect Pie Crust (recipe on page 16), made with ¼ teaspoon ground cinnamon added to the dry ingredients

¼ cup soy milk

*This ABC (Apple Blackberry Cherry) Pie is as easy as 1-2-3, but its flavors are far from elementary.*

1. Preheat the oven to 350°F. Generously grease a 12-cup muffin tin with butter or cooking spray.

2. Combine the apple, blackberries, and cherries in a bowl. Mix in the ⅓ cup sugar, cornstarch, lemon juice, vanilla, and cinnamon. Let sit for 10 minutes to bring out the fruit juices.

3. On a thoroughly floured surface, roll out the pie crust to a thickness of ³⁄₁₆ inch. Using a 4-inch-diameter round cutter, cut 12 crusts. Re-form and re-roll the dough as necessary, keeping plenty of flour on your work surface.

4. Using a mini cookie cutter (your choice) and leftover dough, cut out 12 shapes to use as pie toppers. (We like to use stars for ABC Pie.)

5. Carefully shape the crusts into the wells of the muffin tin, crimping the edges with your fingers.

6. Fill each mini pie with 1½ tablespoons of the fruit mixture. Make sure that each pie gets at least one blackberry and one cherry. Top each pie with a pie topper.

7. With a pastry brush, lightly brush the pie crusts with soy milk, then sprinkle with sugar.

8. Bake for 30 to 35 minutes, until the crusts are golden brown. Allow to cool for a few minutes in the muffin tin, then carefully remove the pies from the pan and place on a wire rack to finish cooling. To remove, first try to spin the pies in the muffin wells. If they need a little extra help, run a butter knife along the edge of the crusts to pop them out of the tin.

9. Serve, or store in an airtight container at room temperature for up to 2 days.

SWEET TIPS: *Be sure to chop the apple to a fine ¼-inch dice to minimize settling during baking.*

*Blackberries tend to burst while baking, so avoid overfilling your mini pies.*

# APPLE CHAI

*An apple chai a day keeps the doctor away.*

1. Preheat the oven to 350°F. Generously grease a 12-cup muffin tin with butter or cooking spray.

2. Combine the apples, brown sugar, granulated sugar, cinnamon, cardamom, allspice, vanilla, and lemon juice in a large bowl. Let sit for 10 minutes to allow the flavors to blend.

3. On a thoroughly floured surface, roll out the pie crust to a thickness of 3/16 inch. Using a 4-inch-diameter round cutter, cut 12 crusts. Re-form and re-roll the dough as necessary, keeping plenty of flour on your work surface.

4. Using the mini cookie cutter of your choice and leftover pie crust, cut out 12 shapes to use as pie toppers. (We like stars for Apple Chai pies.)

5. Carefully shape the crusts into the wells of the muffin tin, crimping the edges with your fingers.

6. Fill each mini pie with 1½ tablespoons of the apple mixture. The filling will settle while baking,

2 apples peeled, cored, and diced into ¼-inch pieces (we like Granny Smith for this pie)

¼ cup brown sugar

¼ cup granulated sugar, plus extra for sprinkling

½ teaspoon ground cinnamon

⅛ teaspoon ground cardamom

¼ teaspoon ground allspice

1 teaspoon vanilla extract

1 tablespoon lemon juice

Perfect Pie Crust (recipe on page 16)

¼ cup soy milk

*sure to dice the apples*
*to a fine ¼-inch dice*
*to minimize settling*
*during baking.*

*For extra flavor, you*
*can add I teaspoon*
*of ground cinnamon*
*to the dry ingredients*
*for the pie crust.*

so it's best to fill the pies higher than the top of the muffin tin. Top each mini pie with a pie topper.

**7.** With a pastry brush, lightly brush the pie crusts with soy milk, then sprinkle with sugar.

**8.** Bake for 20 to 25 minutes, until the crusts are golden brown. Allow to cool for a few minutes in the muffin tin, then carefully remove the pies from the tin and place on a wire rack to finish cooling. To remove, first try to spin the pies in the muffin wells. If they need a little extra help, run a butter knife along the edge of the crusts to pop them out of the tin.

**9.** Serve, or store in an airtight container at room temperature for up to 2 days.

# SPICED CRANBERRY PEAR

*Think fireside chats and spicy cider, in pie form.*

1. Preheat the oven to 350°F. Generously grease a 12-cup muffin tin with butter or cooking spray.

2. Coarsely chop the cranberries until nearly all of them have been cut in half.

3. In a large bowl, combine the cranberries, pears, brown sugar, nutmeg, cloves, allspice, and lemon juice.

4. On a thoroughly floured surface, roll out the pie crust to a thickness of $3/16$ inch. Using a 4-inch-diameter round cutter, cut 12 crusts. Re-form and re-roll the dough as necessary, keeping plenty of flour on your work surface.

5. Using a mini cookie cutter (your choice) and leftover dough, cut out 12 shapes to use as pie toppers. (We like gingerbread-men toppers for Spiced Cranberry Pear pie.)

3 pears*, peeled, cored, and diced in ¼-inch pieces

¾ cup fresh or frozen and thawed cranberries

¼ cup brown sugar

¼ teaspoon ground nutmeg

¼ teaspoon ground cloves

¼ teaspoon ground allspice

1 tablespoon lemon juice

Perfect Pie Crust (recipe on page 16)

¼ cup soy milk

Sugar, for sprinkling

* *For best flavor, mix different types of pears. Our favorites are Bosc and Anjou.*

**SWEET TIPS**: *If your pears are extra juicy, strain out some of the liquid as you fill the mini pies. This will help keep them from boiling over. Surprisingly, there is such a thing as a pie that's too juicy.*

*For extra flavor, add 1 teaspoon of ground cinnamon to the dry ingredients when you make the crust for this pie.*

**6.** Carefully shape the crusts into the wells of the muffin tin, crimping the edges with your fingers.

**7.** Fill each mini pie with 2 tablespoons of the pear mixture, making sure that the cranberries are evenly distributed. This pie is prone to boiling over, so don't include too much of the juice with the filling. Top each mini pie with a pie topper.

**8.** With a pastry brush, lightly brush each pie crust with soy milk, then sprinkle with sugar.

**9.** Bake for 20 to 25 minutes, until the crusts are golden brown. Allow to cool for a few minutes in the muffin tin, then carefully remove the pies from the tin and place on a wire rack to finish cooling. To remove, first try to spin the pies in the muffin wells. If they need a little extra help, run a butter knife along the edge of the crusts to pop them out of the tin.

**10.** Serve, or store in an airtight container at room temperature for up to 2 days.

# BLACKBERRY PEAR

3 pears*, peeled,
cored, and diced
in ¼-inch pieces

1 tablespoon lemon juice

½ teaspoon ground
cinnamon

¼ cup sugar, plus
extra for sprinkling

Perfect Pie Crust
(recipe on page 16)

1 cup fresh or frozen
blackberries

¼ cup soy milk

* For best flavor, mix
different types of
pears. Our favorites
are Bosc and Anjou.

*Bursts of blackberry flavor nestled in pear heaven.*

1. Preheat the oven to 350°F. Generously grease a 12-cup muffin tin with butter or cooking spray.

2. Combine the pears, lemon juice, cinnamon, and sugar in a large bowl. Let sit for 10 minutes to allow the flavors to blend.

3. On a thoroughly floured surface, roll out the pie crust to a thickness of ³⁄₁₆ inch. Using a 4-inch-diameter round cutter, cut 12 crusts. Re-form and re-roll the dough as necessary, keeping plenty of flour on your work surface.

4. Using a mini cookie cutter (your choice) and leftover dough, cut out 12 shapes to use as pie toppers. (We like hearts for Blackberry Pear pie.)

5. Carefully shape the crusts into the wells of the muffin tin, crimping the edges with your fingers.

6. Place two whole blackberries in each mini pie, leaning them vertically against the sides of the crusts. Then fill each mini pie with 1 heaping

tablespoon of the pear mixture. Top each pie with a pie topper.

7. With a pastry brush, lightly brush the pie crusts with soy milk, then sprinkle with sugar.

8. Bake for 20 to 25 minutes, until the crusts are golden brown. Allow to cool for a few minutes in the muffin tin, then carefully remove each pie from the muffin tin and place on a wire rack to finish cooling. To remove, first try to spin the pies in the muffin wells. If they need a little extra help, run a butter knife along the edge of the crusts to pop them out of the tin.

9. Serve, or store in an airtight container at room temperature for up to 2 days.

SWEET TIPS: *Make sure that the blackberries are partially buried by the pear mixture. The blackberries will explode while cooking, giving each mini pie a gorgeous purple color.*

# GINGER PEACH

◇◇◇◇◇◇◇◇◇◇◇◇◇◇◇◇◇◇◇◇◇◇◇◇◇◇

*A favorite of our own Ginger Peach, Miss Morgan Greenseth.*

1. Preheat the oven to 350°F. Generously grease a 12-cup muffin tin with butter or cooking spray.

2. Combine the peaches, brown sugar, granulated sugar, cinnamon, ginger, lemon juice, vanilla, and cornstarch in a large saucepan. Simmer over medium heat, stirring occasionally, for 10 minutes, until bubbly.

3. On a thoroughly floured surface, roll out the pie crust to a thickness of $\frac{3}{16}$ inch. Using a 4-inch-diameter round cutter, cut 12 crusts. Re-form and re-roll the dough as necessary, keeping plenty of flour on your work surface.

4. Using a mini cookie cutter (your choice) and leftover dough, cut out 12 shapes to use as pie toppers. (We like to use stars for Ginger Peach pie.)

5. Carefully shape the crusts into the wells of the muffin tin, crimping the edges with your fingers.

3 not-quite-ripe peaches, peeled and diced in ¼-inch pieces

¼ cup brown sugar

⅛ cup granulated sugar, plus extra for sprinkling

½ teaspoon ground cinnamon

1 teaspoon ground ginger

2 tablespoons lemon juice

1 teaspoon vanilla extract

2 tablespoons cornstarch

Perfect Pie Crust (recipe on page 16)

¼ cup soy milk

**6.** Fill each mini pie with 2 tablespoons of the peach mixture. Don't include too much of the juice with the filling, as this pie is prone to boiling over. Top each mini pie with a pie topper.

**7.** With a pastry brush, lightly brush the pie crusts with soy milk, then sprinkle with sugar.

**8.** Bake for 20 to 25 minutes, until the crusts are golden brown. Allow to cool in the muffin tin for a few minutes, then carefully remove the pies from the pan and place on a wire rack to finish cooling. To remove, first try to spin the pies in the muffin wells. If they need a little extra help, run a butter knife along the edge of the crusts to pop them out of the tin.

**9.** Serve, or store in an airtight container at room temperature for up to 2 days.

# PRETTY PRETTY PLUM

*This plus a glass of wine and you'll be feeling pretty plum good.*

1. Preheat the oven to 375°F. Generously grease a 12-cup muffin tin with butter or cooking spray.

2. Combine the fresh and dried plums, brown sugar, flour, cinnamon, ginger, nutmeg, and pepper in a large bowl.

3. On a thoroughly floured surface, roll out the crust to a thickness of ³⁄₁₆ inch. Using a 4-inch-diameter round cutter, cut 12 crusts. Re-form and re-roll the dough as necessary, keeping plenty of flour on your work surface.

4. Using a mini cookie cutter (your choice) and leftover dough, cut out 12 shapes to use as pie toppers. (We like hearts for topping our Pretty Pretty Plum pie.)

5. Carefully shape the crusts into the wells of the muffin tin, crimping the edges with your fingers.

3 large plums, peeled, pitted, and diced in ¼-inch pieces (about 2½ cups diced)

⅓ cup pitted dried plums, finely chopped

5 tablespoons brown sugar

1½ tablespoons all-purpose flour

⅛ teaspoon ground cinnamon

⅛ teaspoon ground ginger

⅛ teaspoon ground nutmeg

⅛ teaspoon black pepper

Perfect Pie Crust (recipe on page 16)

¼ cup soy milk

Granulated sugar, for sprinkling

6. Fill each mini pie to the brim with the plum mixture. Top each mini pie with a pie topper.

7. With a pastry brush, lightly brush the pie crusts with soy milk, then sprinkle with sugar.

8. Bake for 20 to 25 minutes, until the crusts are golden brown. Allow to cool for a few minutes in the muffin tin, then carefully remove the pies from the pan and place on a wire rack to finish cooling. To remove, first try to spin the pies in the muffin wells. If they need a little extra help, run a butter knife along the edge of the crusts to pop them out of the tin.

9. Serve, or store in an airtight container at room temperature for up to 2 days.

# SAINT GRAPE

1 pound seedless
green grapes

½ cup sugar, plus
extra for sprinkling

2 tablespoons
lemon juice

2 tablespoons
honey

¼ teaspoon
ground nutmeg

2 tablespoons St-
Germain liqueur

⅛ teaspoon salt

2 tablespoons cornstarch

Perfect Pie Crust
(recipe on page 16)

¼ cup soy milk

*Don't knock it 'til you've tried it. Would we lead you astray? One key ingredient—elderflower liqueur—makes this pie heavenly.*

1. Preheat the oven to 425°F. Generously grease a 12-cup muffin tin with butter or cooking spray.

2. Combine the grapes, ½ cup sugar, lemon juice, honey, nutmeg, and St-Germain in a saucepan over medium heat. Bring to a boil to dissolve the sugar, stirring frequently. Remove from heat and stir in the salt and cornstarch.

3. On a thoroughly floured surface, roll out the crust to a thickness of ³⁄₁₆ inch. Using a 4-inch-diameter round cutter, cut 12 crusts. Re-form and re-roll the dough as necessary, keeping plenty of flour on your work surface.

4. Using a mini cookie cutter (your choice) and leftover dough, cut out 12 shapes to use as pie toppers. (We like to top each Saint Grape pie with three ¼-inch circles.)

**5.** Carefully shape the crusts into the wells of the muffin tin, crimping the edges with your fingers.

**6.** Fill each mini pie to the brim with grapes, straining away the liquid. Then go back and add 1½ tablespoons of the liquid to each pie. Top each mini pie with a pie topper.

**7.** With a pastry brush, lightly brush the pie crusts with soy milk, then sprinkle with sugar.

**8.** Bake for 20 to 25 minutes, until the crusts are golden brown. Allow to cool for a few minutes in the muffin tin, then carefully remove the pies from the pan and place on a wire rack to finish cooling. To remove, first try to spin the pies in the muffin wells. If they need a little extra help, run a butter knife along the edge of the crusts to pop them out of the tin.

**9.** Serve, or store in an airtight container at room temperature for up to 2 days.

**SWEET TIPS:** *Grapes soak up flavor just like apples do, and they make an interesting filling for pie. If you don't happen to have St-Germain, add a pinch of ground cardamom and use only 1½ tablespoons cornstarch to make a pie that's a bit more tart.*

# CREAMY CUSTARD PIES

This is where it gets a little more involved. There's a reason why grandmothers are known for making this kind of pie—they've mastered the art of patience. But custard pies are well worth the extra effort. These recipes are listed in order of difficulty, starting with the easiest. Begin with pumpkin and work your way up to decadent, chocolaty heaven, or a delightful dirty chai. It's a delicious trip.

# PUMPKIN

❦❦❦❦❦❦❦❦❦❦❦❦❦❦❦❦❦❦❦❦❦❦❦❦

*Not just for Pilgrims anymore.*

Perfect Pie Crust
(recipe on page 16)

1 large egg

8 ounces canned
solid-pack pumpkin

½ cup heavy
whipping cream

1 teaspoon
vanilla extract

¼ cup sugar, plus
extra for sprinkling

½ teaspoon coarse salt

½ teaspoon ground
cinnamon

¼ teaspoon
ground ginger

¼ teaspoon
ground allspice

¼ cup soy milk

1. Preheat the oven to 325°F. Generously grease a 12-cup muffin tin with butter or cooking spray.

2. On a thoroughly floured surface, roll out the crust to a thickness of 3/16 inch. Using a 4-inch-diameter round cutter, cut 12 crusts. Re-form and re-roll the dough as necessary, keeping plenty of flour on your work surface. For this pie, you want the crusts to be slightly larger than normal. Cut them out as usual, then (working on the floured surface) tap around the edges with the heel of your hand to stretch each crust slightly.

3. Using a mini cookie cutter (your choice) and leftover dough, cut out 12 shapes to use as pie toppers. (We like gingerbread-men toppers for Pumpkin Pie.)

4. Carefully shape the crusts into the wells of the muffin tin, crimping the edges with your fingers, and folding them out over the top of the pan. This will help prevent the crusts from shrinking while

baking. Pierce the bottom of each mini crust with a fork. Bake until lightly golden, 10 to 12 minutes.

5. Meanwhile, lightly beat the egg in a large bowl. Add the pumpkin, cream, vanilla, ¼ cup sugar, salt, cinnamon, ginger, and allspice.

6. Fill each prebaked crust with 1½ tablespoons of the pumpkin mixture, filling almost to the brim. Top each mini pie with a pie topper.

7. With a pastry brush, lightly brush the crust of each pie with soy milk, then sprinkle with sugar.

8. Bake for 30 to 35 minutes, until the crusts are golden brown and the pumpkin filling has firmed up. Allow to cool for a few minutes in the muffin tin, then carefully remove the pies from the pan and place on a wire rack to finish cooling. To remove, first try to spin the pies in the muffin wells. If they need a little extra help, run a butter knife along the edge of the crusts to pop them out of the tin.

9. Serve, or refrigerate in an airtight container for up to 2 days.

# TART KEY LIME

*So refreshingly tart, you'll think you're in Florida.*

1. Preheat the oven to 350°F. Generously grease a 12-cup muffin tin with butter or cooking spray.

2. Thoroughly flour your work surface and sprinkle generously with fine graham cracker crumbs. Roll out the pie crust to a thickness of ³⁄₁₆ inch. Using a 4-inch-diameter round cutter, cut 12 crusts. Re-form and re-roll the dough as necessary, keeping plenty of flour and graham cracker crumbs on your work surface. For this pie, you want the crusts to be slightly larger than normal. Cut them out as usual, then (working on the floured surface) tap around the edges with the heel of your hand to stretch each crust slightly.

3. Carefully shape the crusts into the wells of the muffin tin, crimping the edges with your fingers, and folding them out over the top of the pan. This will help prevent the crusts from shrinking while baking. Pierce the bottom of each mini crust with a fork. Bake until lightly golden, 10 to 12 minutes.

I cup fine graham cracker crumbs (ground in a food processor), for rolling out the crust

Graham Cracker Pie Crust (recipe on page 18)

7 ounces sweetened condensed milk

7 ounces coconut milk

2 limes, yielding I tablespoon zest and 2 tablespoons juice

¼ cup bottled Key lime juice

4 large egg yolks (reserve whites for the meringue)

Perfect Mini Meringue (recipe on page 122)

2 tablespoons sweetened shaved coconut

4. Meanwhile, combine the condensed milk, coconut milk, lime zest, lime juice, Key lime juice, and egg yolks in a large bowl. Whisk until well blended.

5. Fill each prebaked crust to the brim with the lime mixture. (The filling will settle a little while the pies bake.)

6. Bake the pies for 20 minutes.

7. Allow the pies to cool in the pan for 5 minutes. While they cool, make the Perfect Mini Meringue.

8. Spoon the meringue into a pastry bag and pipe onto each pie. Top with coconut shavings.

9. Bake for an additional 10 to 15 minutes, until the meringue is lightly browned. Allow to cool in the muffin tin for a few minutes, then carefully remove the pies from the pan and place on a wire rack to finish cooling. To remove, first try to spin the pies in the muffin wells. If they need a little extra help, run a butter knife along the edge of the crusts to pop them out of the tin.

10. Serve, or refrigerate in an airtight container for up to 2 days.

SWEET TIPS: *It matters! Buy real Key lime juice in a bottle; you'll find it near the lemon juice at the grocery store. You can spend an afternoon juicing little Key limes, but be warned: You'll need about 24 of them to get the ¼ cup of juice you need for this recipe. Just buy the bottle. It's not cheating—it's practical and efficient.*

*The tartness of this filling tends to increase the next day. If you can, bake the night before and store the pies overnight in the refrigerator.*

*You can freeze any leftover pie filling for later use.*

# SUE'S PINK LEMONADE

½ cup strawberries

¼ cup raspberries

¼ cup lemon juice

1 cup fine graham cracker crumbs (ground in a food processor), for rolling out the crust

Graham Cracker Pie Crust (recipe on page 18)

Classic Whipped Cream (recipe on page 118)

2 tablespoons sweetened condensed milk

Colored sprinkles

*It could only be more delicious if you were enjoying it on a screened-in Southern porch.*

1. Preheat the oven to 350°F. Generously grease a 12-cup muffin tin with butter or cooking spray.

2. Coarsely chop the strawberries and raspberries. Combine in a bowl with the lemon juice and allow to sit for 30 minutes. Then place in a food processor and blend to make the pink lemonade.

3. Thoroughly flour your work surface and sprinkle generously with graham cracker crumbs. Roll out the pie crust to a thickness of ³⁄₁₆ inch. Using a 4-inch-diameter round cutter, cut 12 crusts. Re-form and re-roll the dough as necessary, keeping plenty of flour and graham cracker crumbs on your work surface. For this pie, you want the crusts to be slightly larger than normal. Cut them out as usual, then (working on the floured surface) tap around the edges with the heel of your hand to stretch each crust slightly.

4. Carefully shape the crusts into the wells of the muffin tin, crimping the edges with your fingers and folding them out over the top of the pan. This helps prevent the crusts from shrinking while they bake. Pierce the bottom of each mini crust with a fork. Bake for 35 minutes, until lightly browned. Allow to cool in the pan for at least 10 minutes.

5. Meanwhile, chill the whisk and bowl attachment of the electric mixer in the refrigerator for 30 minutes, then make the Classic Whipped Cream.

6. Fold together the pink lemonade, condensed milk, and ¾ of the whipped cream in a large bowl. When the crusts are completely cool, fill them to the brim with the filling mixture.

7. Spoon the remaining homemade whipped cream into a pastry bag and pipe a tiny dollop of whipped cream onto each mini pie. Top with sprinkles. Chill for at least 1 hour.

8. Serve, or refrigerate in an airtight container for up to 2 days.

# MANGO CREAM

*The way to a Mango's heart is through his stomach.*

1. In a food processor, blend the mango, water, and sugar to make mango nectar.

2. In a saucepan over medium heat, whisk together the mango nectar, egg yolks, cream, sugar, cornstarch, and salt. Heat to a boil and whisk for 1 more minute, until the mixture has thickened. Remove from heat and stir in the butter and vanilla. Let cool to room temperature.

3. Preheat the oven to 350°F. Generously grease a 12-cup muffin tin with butter or cooking spray.

4. On a thoroughly floured work surface, roll out the pie crust to a thickness of 3/16 inch. Using a 4-inch-diameter round cutter, cut 12 crusts. Reform and re-roll the dough as necessary, keeping plenty of flour on your work surface. For this pie, you want the crusts to be slightly larger than normal. Cut them out as usual, then (working on the floured surface) tap around the edges of the crusts with the heel of your hand to stretch them slightly.

1 mango, peeled and diced

½ cup water

¼ cup sugar

2 egg yolks

½ cup heavy whipping cream

¼ cup sugar

2½ tablespoons cornstarch

Pinch of salt

1 tablespoon butter

1 teaspoon vanilla extract

Perfect Pie Crust (recipe on page 16)

Coconut Whipped Cream (recipe on page 119)

5. Carefully shape the crusts into the wells of the muffin tin, crimping the edges with your fingers and folding them out over the top of the pan. This will prevent the crusts from shrinking while they bake. Pierce the bottom of each mini crust with a fork. Bake for 30 minutes, until lightly browned. Allow to cool completely

6. Fill each crust with 2 tablespoons of the mango cream. Chill in the refrigerator, covered, for 8 hours in the muffin tin to set the filling.

7. When the pies are set, make the Coconut Whipped Cream.

8. Carefully remove the mini pies from the muffin tin. To remove, first try to spin the pies in the muffin wells. If they need a little extra help, run a butter knife along the edge of the crusts to pop them out of the tin.

9. Spoon the whipped cream into a pastry bag and pipe a tiny dollop onto each chilled mini pie. Serve, or refrigerate in an airtight container for up to 2 days.

# SUSANNE'S LEMON MERINGUE

<>==<>==<>==<>==<>==<>==<>==<>==<>==<>==<>

*Listen to Susanne—she knows lemon meringue. And she's always right.*

1. Preheat the oven to 350°F. Generously grease a 12-cup muffin tin with butter or cooking spray.

2. On a thoroughly floured surface, roll out the crust to a thickness of 3/16 inch. Using a 4-inch-diameter round cutter, cut 12 crusts. Re-form and re-roll the dough as necessary, keeping plenty of flour on your work surface. For this pie, you want the crusts to be slightly larger than normal. Cut them out as usual, then (working on the floured surface) tap around the edges of each crust with the heel of your hand to stretch it slightly.

3. Carefully shape the crusts into the wells of the muffin tin, crimping the edges with your fingers and folding them out over the top of the pan. This will help prevent the crusts from shrinking while they bake. Pierce the bottom of each mini crust with a fork. Bake for 20 minutes, until lightly

Perfect Pie Crust (recipe on page 16)

¾ cup sugar

2½ tablespoons cornstarch

⅛ teaspoon salt

¾ cup water

2 eggs yolks, lightly beaten (reserve the whites for the meringue)

1 tablespoon freshly grated lemon zest

1 tablespoon butter

2 tablespoons lemon juice

Perfect Mini Meringue (recipe on page 122)

browned. Allow to cool in the pan for at least 10 minutes.

**4.** In a saucepan, combine the sugar, cornstarch, and salt. Gradually whisk in the water. Bring the mixture to a boil, stirring constantly, over medium heat. Let boil for exactly 1 minute; the mixture will be thickened but clear.

**5.** Remove from the heat and stir a small amount of the hot liquid into the egg yolks, then whisk the yolks into the mixture in the saucepan. Stir in the lemon zest. Bring to a boil again, stirring constantly, over medium heat. Boil for exactly 1 minute.

**6.** Remove from the heat. Add the butter and stir until melted. Gradually stir in the lemon juice.

**7.** Pour 1½ to 2 tablespoons of the lemon filling into each crust, filling the crust almost to the brim. The filling will set as it cools.

**8.** While the filling cools, make the Perfect Mini Meringue. Spoon the meringue into a pastry bag and pipe onto each pie. Bake for an additional 10 to 15 minutes at 350°F, until the meringue is lightly browned.

10. Allow to cool for a few minutes in the muffin tin, then carefully remove the pies from the pan and place on a wire rack to finish cooling. To remove, first try to spin the pies in the muffin wells. If they need a little extra help, run a butter knife along the edge of the crusts to pop them out of the tin.

11. Serve, or refrigerate in an airtight container for up to 2 days.

# AUNT JIMMA'S CHOCOLATE CREAM

<><><><><><><><><><><><><><><><><><><><><><><><>

*Pie so rich and delightful, you'll think someone's grand-mother made it.*

1. Preheat the oven to 350°F. Generously grease a 12-cup muffin tin with butter or cooking spray.

2. On a thoroughly floured surface, roll out the crust to a thickness of ³⁄₁₆ inch. Using a 4-inch-diameter round cutter, cut 12 crusts. Re-form and re-roll the dough as necessary, keeping plenty of flour on your work surface. For this pie, you want the crusts to be slightly larger than normal. Cut them out as usual, then (working on the floured surface) tap around the edges of each crust with the heel of your hand to stretch it slightly.

3. Carefully shape the crusts into the wells of the muffin tin, crimping the edges with your fingers and folding them out over the top of the pan. This will help prevent the crusts from shrinking while they bake. Pierce the bottom of each mini crust with a fork. Bake for 20 minutes, until lightly

Perfect Pie Crust
(recipe on page 16)

1½ tablespoons
all-purpose flour

1½ tablespoons
unsweetened
cocoa powder

¾ cup sugar

1½ egg yolks
(reserve the whites
for the meringue)

¾ cup PET
evaporated milk

¼ cup whole milk

2 tablespoons butter

1 teaspoon
vanilla extract

browned. Allow to cool in the pan for at least 10 minutes.

4. Meanwhile, stir together the flour, cocoa powder, and sugar in a saucepan. Stir in the egg yolks, evaporated milk, whole milk, butter, and vanilla. Cook over low heat, whisking constantly, until thickened, about 35 minutes. When the mixture is ready, it should coat the back of a spoon and look like chocolate pudding.

5. Pour the hot chocolate mixture into the pre-baked pie crusts, filling each one to the brim. Allow to cool for 5 minutes.

6. Meanwhile, make the Perfect Mini Meringue and spoon it into a pastry bag. Top each pie with meringue and bake for 10 to 15 minutes at 350°F, until the meringue is lightly browned. Allow to cool in the tin for a few minutes, then carefully remove the pies from the pan and place on a wire rack to cool. To remove, spin the pies in the muffin wells. If they need extra help, run a butter knife along the edge to pop them out of the tin.

7. Serve, or refrigerate in an airtight container for up to 2 days.

**SWEET TIPS**: We *know that 35 minutes is a long time to stand and stir, so we have some suggestions for how to keep busy. Call your mother, she worries. Call your grandmother and ask her how she makes chocolate pie. Turn on some music and dance, whisk in hand.*

*Other canned evaporated milks are not the same thing as PET brand milk. PET is the best choice for this recipe, but in a pinch you can use other evaporated milk and still achieve delicious results.*

# PEANUT BUTTER CREAM

◇◇◇◇◇◇◇◇◇◇◇◇◇◇◇◇◇◇◇◇◇◇◇◇◇◇◇◇◇◇◇◇

*This vegan treat is a fluffy, nutty dream.*

Vegan Pie Crust
(recipe on page 20)

I can unsweetened
full-fat coconut milk,
refrigerated overnight

I cup powdered sugar

I teaspoon
vanilla extract

I cup peanut butter
(either creamy or
crunchy—just skim
off any excess oil)

Vegan Whipped Cream
(recipe page 121)

1. Preheat the oven to 350°F. Generously grease a 12-cup muffin tin with vegan buttery sticks or margarine.

2. On a thoroughly floured surface, roll out the crust to a thickness of ³⁄₁₆ inch. Using a 4-inch-diameter round cutter, cut 12 crusts. Re-form and re-roll the dough as necessary, keeping plenty of flour on your work surface. For this pie, you want the crusts to be slightly larger than normal. Cut them out as usual, then (working on the floured surface) tap around the edges of each crust with the heel of your hand to stretch it slightly.

3. Carefully shape the crusts into the wells of the muffin tin, crimping the edges with your fingers and folding them out over the top of the pan. This will help prevent the crusts from shrinking while they bake. Pierce the bottom of each mini crust with a fork. Bake for 20 minutes, until lightly browned. Allow to cool completely.

*For even more nutty flavor, top the whipped cream with chopped peanuts.*

*For a chocolate nutty pie, substitute Nutella for ¼ cup of the peanut butter.*

4. For the filling, open one can of the coconut milk and skim off the cream that has separated; set aside. (Discard the coconut water.) Place the coconut milk in the bowl of an electric mixer with the whisk attachment and beat at high speed until thick and fluffy.

5. With the mixer running, gradually add ½ cup powdered sugar, beating until fully incorporated. Add the vanilla and beat for another 3 to 5 minutes.

6. Beat in ½ cup peanut butter, then add another ½ cup powdered sugar; mix well. Finally, add the remaining ½ cup peanut butter and beat until creamy.

7. Spread about 2 tablespoons of the filling in each cooled pie crust.

8. While the filling sets, make the Vegan Whipped Cream. Spoon into a pastry bag and pipe a healthy dollop onto each mini pie.

9. Serve, or refrigerate in an airtight container for up to 2 days.

# DIRTY CHAI

◇◇◇◇◇◇◇◇◇◇◇◇◇◇◇◇◇◇◇◇◇◇◇◇◇◇◇◇◇◇

*Embracing the coffee culture in our beloved Emerald City.*
*And our inner hippie.*

1. Preheat the oven to 350°F. Generously grease a 12-cup muffin tin with butter or cooking spray.

2. Thoroughly flour your work surface and sprinkle generously with graham cracker crumbs. Roll out the pie crust to a thickness of ³⁄₁₆ inch. Using a 4-inch diameter round cutter, cut 12 crusts. Reform and re-roll the dough as necessary, keeping plenty of flour and graham crackers on your work surface. For this pie, you want the crusts to be slightly larger than normal. Cut them out as usual, then (working on the floured surface) tap around the edges of each crust with the heel of your hand to stretch it slightly.

3. Carefully shape the crusts into the wells of the muffin tin, crimping the edges with your fingers and folding them out over the top of the pan. This will help prevent the crusts from shrinking while they bake. Pierce the bottom of each mini crust with a fork. Bake for 35 minutes, until lightly

1 cup fine graham cracker crumbs (ground in a food processor), for rolling out the crust

Graham Cracker Pie Crust (recipe on page 18)

¼ teaspoon ground cardamom

¼ teaspoon ground cloves

¼ teaspoon ground cinnamon, plus more for dusting

¼ teaspoon ground ginger

1¼ cups reduced-fat (2%) milk, divided

1 chai black tea bag

1 egg

1½ tablespoons cornstarch

Pinch of salt

¼ cup sugar

1 teaspoon fine coffee grounds, plus more for dusting

2 tablespoons butter

Classic Whipped Cream (recipe page 118)

browned. Allow to cool in the pan for at least 10 minutes.

4. While the crusts are baking, make the filling. Combine the cardamom, cloves, cinnamon, ginger, and 1 cup milk in a saucepan. Bring to a boil over medium heat, then remove from the heat. Place the tea bag in the milk mixture, cover, and steep for 15 minutes.

5. In a separate bowl, whisk together the egg, cornstarch, salt, and sugar.

6. Remove the tea bag from the milk mixture, squeezing out all the liquid. Bring the mixture to a boil again. Remove from heat and slowly pour into the egg mixture, whisking constantly. Return the mixture to the saucepan and add the remaining ¼ cup milk and the coffee grounds. Over medium heat, stir until thickened, about 10 minutes. Remove from heat and stir in the butter. Let cool completely.

7. Fill each baked crust with 1 tablespoon of the cooled filling.

8. While the filling is cooling, make the whipped cream.

9. Spoon the whipped cream into a pastry bag and pipe a healthy dollop onto each mini pie. Sprinkle with coffee grounds and a dash of cinnamon.

10. Chill the mini pies for at least 3 hours to set the filling. Serve, or refrigerate in an airtight container for up to 2 days.

SWEET TIPS: *In Seattle, "dirty chai" is chai tea with a shot of espresso. The coffee grounds add a great caffeine kick to this pie. However, they are likely to get stuck in your teeth, so check your pearly whites after indulging in this fabulous little dessert.*

# SAVORY AND NUT PIES

Nut pies are associated with holidays, but are perfect for any occasion. But pies don't always have to be sweet. These savory pies will allow you to double the opportunities to display your impressive repertoire of pie-making skills.

# SAVORY SWEET POTATO
## with Rosemary and Cayenne

½ cup heavy
whipping cream

1 tablespoon packed
fresh rosemary

1 teaspoon ground
cinnamon

Pinch of cayenne pepper

½ teaspoon salt

¼ teaspoon
ground nutmeg

¼ cup brown sugar

Perfect Pie Crust
(recipe on page 16)

1 egg

10 ounces canned
sweet potato

1 teaspoon
vanilla extract

*Spicy and sweet. Just like you. Perfect for the holidays.*

1. Combine the cream, rosemary, cinnamon, cayenne, salt, nutmeg, and brown sugar in a saucepan over low heat; bring to a boil, stirring gently. Let cool, then chill in the refrigerator in an airtight container for 2 hours.

2. Preheat the oven to 350°F. Generously grease a 12-cup muffin tin with butter or cooking spray.

3. On a thoroughly floured surface, roll out the crust to a thickness of ³⁄₁₆ inch. Using a 4-inch-diameter round cutter, cut 12 crusts. Re-form and re-roll the dough as necessary, keeping plenty of flour on your work surface. For this pie, you want the crusts to be slightly larger than normal. Cut them out as usual, then (working on the floured surface) tap around the edges of each crust with the heel of your hand to stretch it slightly.

4. Carefully shape the crusts into the wells of the muffin tin, crimping the edges with your fingers

and folding them out over the top of the pan. This will help prevent the crusts from shrinking while they bake. Pierce the bottom of each mini crust with a fork. Bake for 12 minutes, until lightly browned.

5. Strain the chilled cream mixture and discard the solids, making sure to squeeze all the liquid out first.

6. Lightly beat the egg, then stir together with the cream mixture, sweet potato purée, and vanilla. Fill each mini crust with 2 tablespoons of filling.

7. Bake for 30 minutes, until the crust is lightly browned. Allow to cool in the muffin tin for a few minutes, then carefully remove the pies from the pan and place on a wire rack to finish cooling. To remove, first try to spin the pies in the muffin wells. If they need a little extra help, run a butter knife along the edge of the crusts to pop them out of the tin.

8. Serve, or refrigerate in an airtight container for up to 2 days.

# BOURBON PECAN

*A boozy treat for Turkey Day, or any old day.*

1. Preheat the oven to 350°F. Generously grease a 12-cup muffin tin with butter or cooking spray.

2. On a thoroughly floured surface, roll out the crust to a thickness of ³⁄₁₆ inch. Using a 4-inch-diameter round cutter, cut 12 crusts. Re-form and re-roll the dough as necessary, keeping plenty of flour on your work surface. For this pie, you want the crusts to be slightly larger than normal. Cut them out as usual, then (working on the floured surface) tap around the edges of each crust with the heel of your hand to stretch it slightly.

3. Using a mini cookie cutter (your choice) and leftover dough, cut out 12 shapes to use as pie toppers. (We like crowns to top Bourbon Pecan pie.)

4. Carefully shape the crusts into the wells of the muffin tin, crimping the edges with your fingers and folding them out over the top of the pan. This will help prevent the crusts from shrinking while

Perfect Pie Crust
(recipe on page 16)

1 egg

¼ cup light corn syrup

¼ cup dark corn syrup

⅓ cup sugar

2 tablespoons melted butter

1 tablespoon bourbon (we like Maker's Mark—who doesn't?)

½ teaspoon salt

1¼ cups roughly chopped pecans

they bake. Bake the crusts for 12 minutes, until lightly browned.

5. In a bowl, whisk together the egg, light corn syrup, dark corn syrup, sugar, butter, bourbon, and salt until well combined.

6. Fill each mini crust with ½ tablespoon of the egg mixture. Add chopped pecans, using smaller pieces on the bottom and larger pieces on top. Carefully add another ½ to 1 tablespoon egg mixture to each mini pie, coating the pecans. Fill to just below the brim. Top each mini pie with a pie topper.

7. Bake for 15 minutes, until the crusts are golden brown. Allow to cool in the muffin tin for a few minutes, then carefully remove the pies from the pan and place on a wire rack to finish cooling. To remove, first try to spin the pies in the muffin wells. If they need a little extra help, run a butter knife along the edge of the crusts to pop them out of the tin.

8. Serve, or store in an airtight container for up to 2 days.

SWEET TIPS: *You may as well sip the remaining bourbon while your pies are in the oven.*

*Be sure to completely coat the pecans with the egg mixture. This will ensure that the pie toppers stick and the pecans don't burn.*

# SAVORY APPLE CHILE
## with Cheddar Cheese Crust

3 apples, peeled, cored, and diced in ¼-inch pieces (we like Granny Smith apples for this pie)

¼ cup canned chopped roasted green chiles

1 tablespoon lemon juice

¼ cup granulated sugar

⅛ cup brown sugar

¼ teaspoon ground cinnamon

⅛ teaspoon ground allspice

⅛ teaspoon ground nutmeg

⅛ teaspoon salt

2 tablespoons cornstarch

Cheddar Cheese Pie Crust (recipe on page 23)

*When you just can't decide between sweet and savory, have both!*

1. Preheat the oven to 350°F. Generously grease a 12-cup muffin tin with butter or cooking spray.

2. Combine the apples, chiles, lemon juice, granulated sugar, brown sugar, cinnamon, allspice, nutmeg, and cornstarch in a large bowl. Let sit for 10 minutes to allow the flavors to mingle.

3. In a separate bowl, stir together all the ingredients for the crumb topping.

4. On a thoroughly floured surface, roll out the crust to a thickness of ³⁄₁₆ inch. Using a 4-inch-diameter round cutter, cut 12 crusts. Re-form and re-roll the dough as necessary, keeping plenty of flour on your work surface.

5. Carefully shape the crusts into the wells of the muffin tin, crimping the edges with your fingers.

**6.** Fill each mini pie with 2 tablespoons of the apple mixture. The filling will settle during baking, so it's best to fill the crusts higher than the top of the muffin tin. Top each mini pie with crumb topping.

**7.** Bake for 20 to 25 minutes, until the crusts are golden brown. Allow to cool for a few minutes in the muffin tin, then carefully remove the pies from the pan and place on a wire rack to finish cooling. To remove, first try to spin the pies in the muffin wells. If they need a little extra help, run a butter knife along the edge of the crusts to pop them out of the tin.

**8.** Serve, or store in an airtight container at room temperature for up to 2 days.

FOR THE CRUMB TOPPING:

¼ cup all-purpose flour

¼ cup finely chopped walnuts

⅛ cup light brown sugar

2 tablespoons melted butter

**SWEET TIPS:** *Be sure to finely chop the apples to a ¼-inch dice to minimize settling during baking.*

*This recipe is a real crowd-pleaser—perfect for an event such as a Super Bowl party.*

# DILLED SPINACH CUP-QUICHE

◇◇◇◇◇◇◇◇◇◇◇◇◇◇◇◇◇◇◇◇◇◇◇◇◇◇◇◇◇◇◇◇◇◇

Cheddar Cheese
Pie Crust (recipe
on page 23)

¼ cup crumbled
feta cheese

¼ cup thinly sliced
green onions

¼ cup diced red
bell pepper

Salt and black
pepper

1 egg

¾ cup heavy
whipping cream

½ teaspoon dill
weed

1 cup frozen chopped
spinach, thawed
and drained

*This mini quiche is the perfect pie for a Sunday brunch.*

1. Preheat the oven to 350°F. Generously grease a
12-cup muffin tin with butter or cooking spray.

2. On a thoroughly floured surface, roll out the
crust to a thickness of ³⁄₁₆ inch. Using a 4-inch-
diameter round cutter, cut 12 crusts and pie toppers. Re-form and re-roll the dough as necessary,
keeping plenty of flour on your work surface. For
this pie, you want the crusts to be slightly larger
than normal. Cut them out as usual, then (working on the floured surface) tap around the edges of
each crust with the heel of your hand to stretch it
slightly.

3. Carefully shape the crusts into the wells of the
muffin tin, crimping the edges with your fingers
and folding them out over the top of the pan. This
will help prevent the crusts from shrinking while
they bake. Pierce the bottom of each crust with a
fork. Bake the crusts for 12 minutes, until lightly
browned. Allow to cool.

*Beware of spinach clumps while you are pouring the filling into the crusts. Don't worry if you do happen to overfill a crust—your cup-quiche will still be fine.*

*Although this mini-quiche can be served cold, eating it fresh out of the oven is especially delicious.*

4. Scatter bits of feta, green onions, and peppers in each cooled crust—just enough to cover the bottom. Season to taste with salt and pepper.

5. Whisk the egg in a small bowl, add the cream, and whisk until smooth. Add the dill, a pinch of salt, and a grind of pepper; whisk well. Squeeze any excess moisture from the spinach, then stir it into the egg mixture, mixing well. Transfer the mixture to a glass measuring cup with a pouring spout. Pour over the veggies in each crust, filling each one to the brim.

6. Bake for 45 minutes, until the crusts are golden brown and the top is puffed. Allow to cool for a few minutes in the muffin tin, then carefully remove the quiches from the pan and place on a wire rack to finish cooling. To remove, first try to spin the quiches in the muffin wells. If they need a little extra help, run a butter knife along the edge of the crusts to pop them out of the tin.

7. Serve, or refrigerate in an airtight container for up to 2 days.

# CARAMELIZED ONION, OLIVE, & THYME TART

<><><><><><><><><><><><><><><><><><><>

*How to impress a vegan.*

1. Preheat the oven to 350°F. Generously grease a 12-cup muffin tin with vegan buttery sticks or margarine.

2. Cut half of the onion into thin rings. Dice the remaining half.

3. In a large skillet, heat the olive oil over medium-high heat until hot but not smoking. Reduce the heat to medium and add the onions. Cook for 10 minutes, stirring often. Add the minced garlic and thyme and continue to cook, stirring, until the onions are soft.

4. Sprinkle the sugar over the onions and continue to cook, stirring occasionally, until the onions start to caramelize, about 20 minutes more. Remove from the heat.

5. While the onions are cooking, combine all the tapenade ingredients in a food processor or chop-

1 large onion, peeled

1 tablespoon olive oil

1 clove garlic, peeled and minced

½ teaspoon thyme, plus more for sprinkling

½ teaspoon sugar

Vegan Pie Crust (recipe on page 20)

4 to 6 tablespoons olive tapenade (see ingredients page 105)

per. Blend or chop until the ingredients are finely minced.

6. On a thoroughly floured surface, roll out the crust to a thickness of 3/16 inch. Using a 4-inch-diameter round cutter, cut 12 crusts. Re-form and re-roll the dough as necessary, keeping plenty of flour on your work surface.

7. Using a mini cookie cutter (your choice) and leftover dough sprinkled with thyme, cut out 12 shapes to use as pie toppers. (We like leaf shapes for these.)

8. Carefully shape the crusts into the wells of the muffin tin, crimping the edges with your fingers.

9. Place ½ tablespoon of the tapenade in each pie shell and top with about 2 tablespoons of the onions. Top each pie with a mini pie topper.

10. Bake for 25 to 30 minutes, until the crusts are golden brown.

11. Serve immediately, or refrigerate in an airtight container for up to 2 days. To reheat, preheat the oven to 350°F and bake for 10 minutes or until warm.

FOR THE TAPENADE:

¼ cup pitted black olives

¼ cup pitted green olives

½ tablespoon capers (optional)

I clove garlic, peeled and crushed

I tablespoon olive oil

I teaspoon lemon juice

Black pepper to taste

SAVORY TIPS: *You can use store-bought tapenade, but why would you when it's so simple to make your own? This is a great appetizer for your vegan friends. It's best served the day you make it, but you probably won't have leftovers anyway.*

# RUM MAPLE HAZELNUT

2 cups hazelnuts

5 tablespoons pure maple syrup

¼ cup brown sugar

¼ cup light corn syrup

¼ teaspoon salt

2 tablespoons butter

1 tablespoon rum (we like Captain Morgan)

½ teaspoon vanilla extract

1 egg

Perfect Pie Crust (recipe on page 16)

*The best things from nature, all in one pie.*

1. Preheat the oven to 350°F. Generously grease a 12-cup muffin tin with butter or cooking spray.

2. Finely chop half of the hazelnuts; set aside.

3. In a saucepan over medium heat, stir together the maple syrup, brown sugar, corn syrup, and salt. Bring to a boil and boil for 1 minute. Remove from heat. Add the butter and rum, stir together, and let cool completely.

4. In a bowl, gently whisk together the vanilla extract and the egg. Stir together with the cooled syrup mixture.

5. On a thoroughly floured surface, roll out the crust to a thickness of ³⁄₁₆ inch. Using a 4-inch-diameter round cutter, cut out 12 crusts. Re-form and re-roll the dough as necessary, keeping plenty of flour on your work surface.

**6.** Using a mini cookie cutter (your choice) and leftover dough, cut out 12 shapes to use as pie toppers.

**7.** Carefully shape the crusts into the wells of the muffin tin, crimping the edges with your fingers.

**8.** Distribute the chopped hazelnuts among the pie crusts. Top with the whole hazelnuts and then pour 1½ tablespoons of filling mixture into each pie. Top each mini pie with a pie topper.

**9.** Bake for 25 to 30 minutes, until the crusts are golden brown. Allow to cool for a few minutes in the muffin tin, then carefully remove the pies from the pan and place on a wire rack to finish cooling. To remove, first try to spin the pies in the muffin wells. If they need a little extra help, run a butter knife along the edge of the crusts to pop them out of the tin.

**10.** Serve, or store in an airtight container at room temperature for up to 2 days.

SWEET TIPS:
*This pie is a twist on the traditional Bourbon Pecan Pie.*

*Hazelnuts are rad—use them more often!*

# ROCKY ROAD

Graham Cracker
Pie Crust (recipe
on page 18)

1 cup fine graham
cracker crumbs (ground
in a food processor), for
rolling out the crust

FOR THE ROCKS:

1¼ cups almonds,
chopped

1¼ cups miniature
marshmallows, chopped

3 ounces semisweet
baking chocolate,
chopped

FOR THE ROAD:

5 ounces semisweet
baking chocolate,
chopped

1 cup heavy
whipping cream

1 egg

*It's not the journey, it's the delicious destination.*

1. Thoroughly flour your work surface and sprinkle generously with graham cracker crumbs. Roll out the crust to a thickness of ³⁄₁₆ inch. Using a 4-inch-diameter round cutter, cut 12 crusts. Re-form and re-roll the dough as necessary, keeping plenty of flour and graham crackers on your work surface. For this pie, you want the crusts to be slightly larger than normal. Cut them out as usual, then (working on the floured surface) tap around the edges with the heel of your hand to stretch them slightly.

2. Carefully form the crusts into the muffin tin, crimping the edges with your fingers and folding the edges out over the top of the pan. This will prevent the crusts from shrinking while they bake. Pierce the bottom of each crust with a fork. Bake for 35 minutes, until the crusts are lightly browned. While the crusts are baking, you can prepare the "rocks" and the "road."

3. Combine all the rocks ingredients in a large bowl; set aside.

*Because the egg in this recipe isn't completely cooked, avoid serving this pie to anyone with a weak immune system, children, or the elderly.*

4. For the chocolate custard road, melt the semi-sweet chocolate in a heatproof bowl set over a saucepan of simmering water. In another saucepan over low heat, heat the cream to a gentle simmer.

5. Whisk the egg in a bowl. Now the tricky part: Stir a tiny bit of the hot cream into the egg, then whisk the egg into the cream in the saucepan. Simmer 5 minutes, stirring continuously. Now add the egg and cream mixture to the chocolate and whisk until well combined. Turn off the heat under the chocolate, but leave the mixture in the bowl over the hot water.

6. Fill each prebaked crust to the brim with the rocks, evenly distributing the marshmallows, almonds, and chocolate. You'll have rocks left over. Very carefully pour 1 tablespoon of the road (the chocolate custard) over the rocks in each pie. Allow to settle, then add another ½ tablespoon of chocolate custard to each pie. Top with the remaining rocks and chill for at least 1 hour.

7. Remove from the pan and serve, or refrigerate in an airtight container for up to 2 days.

# HONEY &
# PINE NUT TART

*A delightfully light treat for you or your honey.*

1. Combine the sugar, honey, and salt in a saucepan over medium heat. Bring to a boil, stirring constantly, until the sugar is completely dissolved. Add the butter gradually and stir until combined. Remove from heat and allow to cool for 30 minutes.

2. Whisk the cream and egg together in a bowl. Slowly pour the cream mixture into the honey mixture, whisking until well combined.

3. Preheat the oven to 325°F. Generously grease a 12-cup muffin tin with butter or cooking spray.

4. On a thoroughly floured surface, roll out the crust to a thickness of 3/16 inch. Using a 4-inch-diameter round cutter, cut 12 crusts. Re-form and re-roll the dough as necessary, keeping plenty of flour on your work surface.

¼ cup granulated sugar

¼ cup honey

1 teaspoon salt

6 tablespoons butter, chopped into ¼-inch pieces

¼ cup heavy whipping cream

1 egg

Shortbread Pie Crust (recipe on page 24)

2¼ cups pine nuts

¼ cup soy milk

**5.** Using a mini cookie cutter (your choice) and leftover dough, cut out 12 shapes to use as pie toppers.

**6.** Carefully shape the crusts into the wells of the muffin tin, crimping the edges with your fingers.

**7.** Spoon 1½ tablespoons of pine nuts into each pie, then add 1 tablespoon of the honey and cream mixture. Add another tablespoon of pine nuts, then ½ tablespoon more of the honey mixture. Top with a few pine nuts and a pie topper. With a pastry brush, lightly brush the crust of each pie with soy milk, then sprinkle with sugar.

**8.** Bake for 35 minutes, until the crusts are browned. Allow to cool in the muffin tin for a few minutes, then carefully remove the pies from the pan and place on a wire rack to finish cooling.

**9.** Serve, or store in an airtight container for up to 2 days.

**SWEET TIPS:** *This delightfully crumbly crust can be challenging. If you roll out the crust and it's too crumbly, use your hands to knead it back into a ball and then roll it out again. The second time around, the dough will be more elastic.*

*You want to be sure that the pine nuts are fully coated with the honey and cream mixture, hence the layering of ingredients. You can fill these little babies right to the brim, as this filling won't boil over.*

# CRANBERRY ALMOND PISTACHIO

½ cup dried cranberries

½ cup slivered almonds

½ cup shelled
raw pistachios

½ cup dark brown sugar

½ cup pure maple syrup

1 tablespoon molasses

2 tablespoons heavy
whipping cream

2 tablespoons
butter

3 egg yolks

Perfect Pie Crust
(recipe on page 16)

1 cup fresh cranberries

¼ cup soy milk

*There's nothing wrong with being a little nutty.*

1. Preheat the oven to 350°F. Generously grease a 12-cup muffin tin with butter or cooking spray.

2. Combine the dried cranberries, almonds, and pistachios in a bowl; set aside.

3. In a saucepan over medium heat, stir together the brown sugar, maple syrup, molasses, cream, and butter. Bring to a boil, then remove from the heat.

4. In a separate heatproof bowl, whisk the egg yolks gently while slowly pouring the hot syrup mixture over them. Whisk until well combined.

5. On a thoroughly floured surface, roll out the crust to a thickness of ³⁄₁₆ inch. Using a 4-inch-diameter round cutter, cut 12 crusts. Re-form and re-roll the dough as necessary, keeping plenty of flour on your work surface.

**6.** Using a mini cookie cutter (your choice) and leftover dough, cut out 12 shapes to use as pie toppers. (We like to use hearts for Cranberry Almond Pistachio pie.)

**7.** Carefully shape the crusts into the wells of the muffin tin, crimping the edges with your fingers.

**8.** Distribute the cranberry and nut mixture among the mini crusts, filling them to just below the brim. Then pour 1½ tablespoons of the syrup and egg mixture into each pie. Distribute the fresh cranberries onto the pies. Top each mini pie with a pie topper. With a pastry brush, lightly brush the crust of each pie with soy milk, then sprinkle with sugar.

**9.** Bake for 25 to 30 minutes, until the crusts are golden brown. Allow to cool for a few minutes in the muffin tin, then carefully remove the pies from the pan and place on a wire rack to finish cooling.

**10.** Serve, or store in an airtight container at room temperature for up to 2 days.

SWEET TIPS: *The fresh cranberries on top add juicy flavor and make these pies especially pretty.*

# TOPPINGS

Little details like garnishes help make food even more appetizing and give it character. For mini pies, toppings are very important to finishing off your tiny baked creations. They can add another layer of flavor, discretely label the filling, and give the pie personality. Whether it's a tiny toasted crust crown, a spiced crumble, or a fluffy meringue, learn how to create these toppings and seal a sweet deal of a pie.

# CLASSIC WHIPPED CREAM

¾ cup heavy whipping cream

2 tablespoons powdered sugar

½ teaspoon vanilla extract

**SWEET TIPS:** *It's easy to over-beat the cream, so keep a close eye on it—you want whipped cream, not butter. The whole process takes only about 2 minutes.*

*A delicious addition to your dessert repertoire.*

1. Chill the whisk attachment and bowl of an electric mixer in the refrigerator for 30 minutes. Then beat the cream until soft peaks form when you lift the beater. With the mixer running, add the powdered sugar and vanilla. Beat until stiff peaks form.

# FLAVORED WHIPPED CREAM

*When you want a touch more flavor.*

1. Chill the whisk attachment and bowl of an electric mixer in the refrigerator for 30 minutes. Then beat the cream until soft peaks form. With the mixer running, add the powdered sugar and your extract of choice. Beat until stiff peaks form.

¾ cup heavy whipping cream

2 tablespoons powdered sugar

½ teaspoon almond, coconut, mint, or lemon extract

**SWEET TIPS:** *For other flavor options, use vanilla extract with ground cinnamon, instant coffee, or cocoa powder (with a touch more sugar).*

# BASIL WHIPPED CREAM

¾ cup heavy whipping cream

½ cup finely chopped and packed fresh basil leaves

2 tablespoons sugar

¾ cup mascarpone cheese

*Something you didn't know you'd been missing out on.*

1. Combine the cream, basil, and sugar in a metal bowl. Place the bowl over a saucepan of simmering water and stir until the sugar dissolves. Cover with plastic wrap and chill for 2 hours to infuse the whipping cream with basil flavor.

2. Chill the whisk attachment and bowl of an electric mixer in the refrigerator for 30 minutes.

3. Strain the solids out of the chilled cream mixture. Combine the cream mixture and the mascarpone cheese in the chilled mixer bowl and beat until stiff peaks form.

# VEGAN WHIPPED CREAM

*A simple, non-dairy whipped topping!*

1. Open the coconut milk, skim off the cream that has separated, and set aside. (Discard the coconut water.) Pour the coconut milk into a mixing bowl and beat on high until fluffy and thick. With the mixer running, add the powdered sugar gradually until it is fully incorporated.

2. Add the vanilla and beat for another 3 to 5 minutes.

2 (15-ounce) cans full-fat coconut milk, refrigerated overnight

⅔ cup powdered sugar

2 teaspoons vanilla extract

**SWEET TIPS:** *Don't throw out the coconut water in the can—drink it as is, or add it to a smoothie.*

# PERFECT MINI MERINGUE

4 egg whites, at room temperature

¼ teaspoon cream of tartar

¼ teaspoon salt

5 tablespoons sugar, or more as needed

*No matter what you've heard, this isn't impossible.*

**1.** Using an electric mixer with the whisk attachment, beat the egg whites until foamy.

**2.** Beat in the cream of tartar and salt.

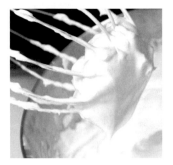

3. Continuing to beat at a high speed, add the sugar 1 tablespoon at a time. Beat well after each addition and continue beating until stiff peaks form, about 5 minutes more.

4. Spread or pipe the meringue onto your mini pies, making sure the pie edges are covered. Then pile high in the center and bake according to the recipe you are using.

*SWEET TIPS: This recipe makes enough for 24 mini pies, great for large gatherings.*

*For piping the prettiest meringues, we like a #22 piping tip with a ¼-inch opening.*

*If you accidentally get some egg yolk in with your whites, use a spoon to remove it. The meringue won't turn out right if there's any yolk in the mixture.*

# CONVERSIONS

| MEASURE | EQUIVALENT | METRIC |
|---|---|---|
| 1 teaspoon | -- | 5 milliliters |
| 1 tablespoon | 3 teaspoons | 14.8 milliliters |
| 1 cup | 16 tablespoons | 236.8 milliliters |
| 1 pint | 2 cups | 473.6 milliliters |
| 1 quart | 4 cups | 947.2 milliliters |
| 1 liter | 4 cups + 3½ tablespoons | 1000 milliliters |
| 1 ounce (dry) | 2 tablespoons | 28.35 grams |
| 1 pound | 16 ounces | 453.49 grams |
| 2.21 pounds | 35.3 ounces | 1 kilogram |
| 325°F/350°F/375°F | -- | 165°C/177°C/190°C |

*Morgan Greenseth (left) and Christy Beaver enjoy a jar pie.*

# ABOUT THE AUTHORS

**CHRISTY BEAVER** was raised in southern Arkansas and began helping her mother and grandmother in the kitchen as soon as she could walk, from which she developed a lifelong love for pie. After moving to the Pacific Northwest, she noticed a lack of wholesome home-baked goods, which inspired her to start Mini Empire Bakery. She has owned her own business designing restaurant, retail, and residential interior spaces. Her goals are to enable Seattleites to enjoy small portions of their favorite treats and to help Mini Empire Bakery take over the world, one tiny dessert at a time. She lives in Seattle, Washington, with her devoted dachshund, Andy.

**MORGAN GREENSETH** has been involved with the many aspects of food throughout her life. Growing up in the Midwest, as a young girl she learned to bake with her mother and grandmother. She now designs the interiors of restaurants and cafés, and also helps fill their pastry case with treats. When not brightening up interiors, she's working on new bite-size recipes for Mini Empire Bakery. She has written about food and the environment for Worldchanging.com and has served as a panelist for the *Fearless Critic Seattle Restaurant Guide* book. Having relocated from Seattle, Washington, to New York City, Morgan is on a mission to expand Mini Empire to the East Coast.